IMAGES
of America

U.S. ARMY NATICK
LABORATORIES
THE SCIENCE BEHIND
THE SOLDIER

THE PACKAGING INSTITUTE, U.S.A.
HONORS THE
U.S. ARMY NATICK LABORATORIES
FOR
A FLEXIBLE PACKAGE & SYSTEM
FOR THERMALLY PROCESSED FOODS

THIS ACCOMPLISHMENT COMPARES IN SIGNIFICANCE TO
THE DEVELOPMENT OF THE CANNING TECHNIQUE BY
NICOLAS APPERT IN 1809 AND IS OF MAJOR BENEFIT TO
THE ARMED FORCES, THE PACKAGING INDUSTRY AND
THE CIVILIAN CONSUMER

OCTOBER 4, 1973

Dated October 4, 1973, this plaque at Natick honors the U.S. Army's development of food-preservation processes as important as the original development of canning by Nicholas Appert in France, under the auspices of Napoleon Bonaparte.

IMAGES
of America

U.S. ARMY NATICK LABORATORIES
THE SCIENCE BEHIND THE SOLDIER

Alan R. Earls

ARCADIA
PUBLISHING

Published by Arcadia Publishing
Charleston, South Carolina

Library of Congress Catalog Card Number: 2004113780

For all general information, contact Arcadia Publishing at:
Telephone 843-853-2070
Fax 843-853-0044
E-mail sales@arcadiapublishing.com
For customer service and orders:
Toll-free 1-888-313-2665

Visit us on the Internet at www.arcadiapublishing.com

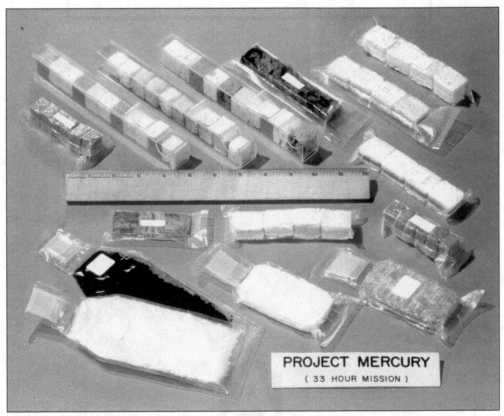

Miniaturized foods were developed by Natick to be used by America's astronauts.

CONTENTS

Acknowledgments

The author is grateful for the help from everyone at the U.S. Army Soldier Systems Center at Natick (the current name for a facility still known popularly as Natick Labs), but particularly, photographer Sarah Underhill; Patricia Welsh, Public Affairs Office; Richard Walunas, chief, Strategic Communications; and Jeremiah Whitaker, chief, Public Affairs Office. All embraced the concept of the book from the moment I suggested it. They were helpful in every way. They provided access to all the images used in this book and permission to reprint them here. In addition to photographs, they also provided me copies of a number of brief histories that have been written about the Natick Labs over the years. Special thanks go out to the anonymous individual who, decades ago, assembled a comprehensive scrapbook detailing the earliest years of the labs. It was an invaluable source of information. Finally, thanks are due to editor Shannan Goff and the other helpful people at Arcadia Publishing for bringing this book to fruition.

While this volume focuses primarily on the important work the Natick Labs undertook on behalf of the government and the important role the facility played in the community, it is important to acknowledge the less positive impact this work had as well. Natick researchers tested and handled a vast range of chemical, biological, and nuclear substances over the years, using safety practices that were typical for the time but often were completely inadequate, when viewed in hindsight. As a result, the Natick Labs site was declared a federal Superfund site in 1994. In addition, groundwater contamination forced the town to build a $4 million water-treatment system in 1997. To its credit, the U.S. Army helped fund this work and has cooperated with investigators since.

INTRODUCTION

The Quartermaster Corps, which spawned today's Soldier Systems Center (commonly known as the Natick Laboratories), traces its origins to June 1775, when the Second Continental Congress passed a resolution that provided for "one Quartermaster General of the grand army and a deputy, under him, for the separate army."

In 1912, the former Subsistence, Pay, and Quartermaster Departments were consolidated into the Quartermaster Corps, which played an important role in sustaining American troops in France a few years later, during World War I. This, however, proved to be only the beginning, as some in the U.S. Army looked at the potential demands of the next conflict. For instance, efforts to develop improved field rations began at the Quartermaster Corps Subsistence Research Laboratory, in Chicago, as early as 1936.

Still, at the start of World War II, the U.S. Army was only beginning the process of equipping troops to fight in terrains as diverse as tropical jungles, deserts, and the arctic conditions of the Aleutians and Alaska. The results of this lack of preparedness included food shipments that went bad on their way to the early campaigns in the South Pacific, and soldiers incapacitated by trench foot and frostbite in colder climates. Fortunately, even before America's entry into World War II, the quartermaster general took steps to expand the technical staff that could anticipate and address such problems. A key step was Maj. Gen. Edmund B. Gregory's recruitment of Georges Doriot, a professor at Harvard Business School. By September 1942, a research-and-development branch was set up in the Office of the Quartermaster General, later supplemented by the Requirements Branch and Operations Branch. This whole became the Military Planning Division, headed by Doriot (a colonel, later brigadier general).

One of the first lab facilities pressed into service by the organization was a cold chamber in Lawrence. Set up by Pacific Mills for the freeze-cleaning of wool, it was used to test clothing and equipment and was quickly supplemented by a hot chamber. Other facilities were developed at Fort Lee, Virginia, and at the Climatic Research Laboratory in Jeffersonville, Indiana. Researchers soon made progress in areas such as developing mildew-resistant material for fabrics.

With the end of the war, it was clear to see that much more could be done, so an organization was assembled under Maj. Gen. W. H. Middleswart. Just as clear, however, was the need to consolidate operations that also included research-and-development facilities in Philadelphia and Chicago. The Boston area was at the top of the list because of its scientific resources and because of the wide range of climatic variations within the region, including the infamous extremes on Mount Washington in New Hampshire. The ceremonial laying of a cornerstone for the Natick facility happened on May 30, 1953, with Speaker Joseph W. Martin Jr., Sen. Leverett Saltonstall, Sen. John F. Kennedy, and others in attendance.

U.S. ARMY SOLDIER SYSTEMS CENTER COMMANDERS

Brig. Gen. James R. Moran
2004–present

Col. David J. Bongi
2003–2004

Brig. Gen. Craig A. Peterson
2002–2003

Col. James L. Kennon
2001–2002

Brig. Gen. Philip M. Mattox
2000–2001

Brig. Gen. J. A. "Yogi" Mangual
1998–2000

Brig. Gen. Robert L. Floyd II
1997–1998

Col. Richard Ross
1996–1997

Col. Henry T. Glisson
1994–1996

Col. Morris E. Price
1993–1994

Col. David H. Wayne
1991–1993

Col. Joseph W. Kernodle
1989–1991

Col. Clinton A. Hodder
1987–1989

Col. A. D. Rogers
1985–1987

Col. David L. Saunders
1983–1985

Col. James S. Hayes
1981–1983

Col. Robert J. Cuthbertson
1979–1981

Col. Hugh F. Penney
1977–1979

Col. Rufus E. Lester Jr.
1974–1977

Col. Harry L. Corkill Jr.
1973–1974

Brig. Gen. John C. McWhorter Jr.
1972–1973

Col. William B. Levin
1971–1972

Brig. Gen. Dean VanLydegraf
1970–1971

Col. Howard James
1969–1970

Brig. Gen. Felix J. Gerace
1968–1969

Col. Clifford T. Riordan
1967–1968

Brig. Gen. William M. Mantz
1966–1967

Brig. Gen. Woodrow W. Vaughan
1964–1966

Brig. Gen. Merrill L. Tribe
1960–1964

Col. Hoke S. Wofford
1960–1960

Maj. Gen. Charles G. Calloway
1954–1960

Brig. Gen. Joseph C. O'Dell
1953–1954

Natick Soldier Center Technical Directors

Philip Brandler	1994–present
Dr. Robert W. Lewis	April 1988–1994
Edward F. Levell	July 1985–March 1988
Dr. Robert T. Byrne	March 1982–July 1985
James H. Flanagan	September 1979–August 1980
Dr. Dale H. Sieling	June 1959–August 1979
Dr. Stuart A. Hunter	October 1953–October 1958

Navy Clothing and Textile Research Facility
Officers in Charge and Directors Since the Move to Natick

Dr. Barbara Avellini	August 1998–present
Cmdr. Daniel R. Smith	October 1997–August 1998
Cmdr. Keith T. Adams	October 1994–October 1997
Dr. Barbara Avellini (Acting)	July 1994–October 1994
Cmdr. William E. Johnson	July 1989–July 1994
Cmdr. Gary R. Peterson	June 1985–July 1989
Cmdr. James C. Robertson	October 1982–June 1985
Cmdr. John B. Sewell	August 1980–October 1982
Cmdr. Donald S. Parsons	May 1977–August 1980
Cmdr. Richard A. J. Ranieri	July 1975–May 1977
Cmdr. Joseph P. Mitts	December 1972–July 1975
Mr. Seymour Lash (Acting)	July 1972–December 1972
Cmdr. John L. Poor	October 1969–July 1972
Lt. Cmdr. John J. Gordon	July 1967–October 1969

U.S. Army Research Institute of Environmental Medicine Commanders

Col. Karl E. Friedl	August 2003–present
Col. John P. Obusek	August 2000–August 2003
Col. David M. Penetar	October 1997–August 2000
Col. Joel T. Hiatt	June 1994–October 1997
Col. Gerald P. Krueger	July 1990–June 1994
Col. Joseph C. Denniston	April 1989–July 1990
Col. David D. Schnakenberg	June 1986–April 1989
Col. Brendan E. Joyce	November 1984–June 1986
Col. Ernest M. Irons Jr.	July 1982–November 1984
Col. Eliot J. Pearlman	July 1980–July 1982
Col. Harry G. Dangerfield	August 1976–July 1980
Col. LeeRoy G. Jones	August 1971–July 1976
Col. James E. Hansen	August 1965–July 1971
Lt. Col. William H. Hall	January 1962–July 1965
Capt. Robert J. T. Joy	July 1961–January 1962

Soldier Systems Center Timeline

October 1949	Construction of Quartermaster Research Laboratory authorized by Congress.
April 1952	Groundbreaking ceremonies.
November 1952	Construction started.
May 1953	Cornerstone-laying ceremonies held.
October 1953	Quartermaster Research Laboratory renamed Quartermaster Research and Development Center, established as Quartermaster Class II installation.
October 1953	Quartermaster Research and Development Command established with headquarters at Quartermaster Research and Development Center, Natick.
October 1954	Dedication held.
January 1957	Quartermaster Research and Development Center redesignated Quartermaster Research and Engineering Command.
July 1961	U.S. Army Research Institute of Environmental Medicine (USARIEM) activated at Natick.
July 1962	Quartermaster Research and Engineering Center placed under U.S. Army Materiel Command (AMC) headquarters.
November 1962	Quartermaster Research and Engineering Center redesignated as Natick Laboratories.
Summer 1963	Food and Container Institute moved to Natick.
July 1967	Navy Clothing and Textile Research Facility moved from Bayonne, N.J., to Natick.
October 1968	USARIEM building dedicated.
May 1971	Earth Sciences Laboratory transferred to chief of engineers, Fort Belvoir, Va.
July 1973	Natick Laboratories made a subordinate element to U.S. Army Troop Support Command (TROSCOM).
March 1975	Natick Laboratories redesignated U.S. Army Natick Development Center and reassigned to commander, AMC.
January 1976	U.S. Army Natick Development Center redesignated U.S. Army Natick Research and Development Command, assigned to commander, U.S. Army Material Development and Readiness Command.
January 1976	AMC redesignated as U.S. Army Development and Readiness Command (DARCOM).
September 1980	U.S. Army Natick Research and Development Command redesignated as U.S. Army Natick Research and Development Laboratories.

October 1983	U.S. Army Natick Research and Development Laboratories redesignated U.S. Army Natick Research and Development Center, subordinate element of TROSCOM, St. Louis.
July 1992	TROSCOM merged with U.S. Army Aviation Systems Command (AVSCOM) to form the U.S. Army Aviation and Troop Command (ATCOM, Provisional). Natick falls under ATCOM.
October 1992	U.S. Army Natick Research, Development and Engineering Center (NRDEC) designated a subordinate element of ATCOM in St. Louis.
November 1994	U.S. Army Soldier Systems Command activated at Natick. Organizations include the U.S. Army Natick Research, Development and Engineering Center; Product Manager–Soldier and Army Support Office.
February 1995	Sustainment and Readiness Directorate established.
October 1995	Product Manager–Soldier Support established.
October 1996	Operations of Clothing and Services Office transferred to Natick from Fort Lee, Va.
June 1997	Product Manager–Force Provider relocated to Natick.
October 1997	Sustainment and Readiness Directorate transitioned into Integrated Materiel Management Center.
October 1998	NRDEC renamed the Natick Soldier Center.
October 1998	Soldier Systems Command merged with Chemical Biological Defense Command into the Soldier and Biological Chemical Command. Installation renamed Soldier Systems Center.
January 2002	Product Manager–Soldier replaced by Program Executive Office–Soldier in Fort Belvoir, Va.
January 2002	Product Manager–Force Sustainment Systems established, replacing Product Manager–Soldier Support and including former Product Manager–Force Provider.
June 2002	Natick Soldier Center realigned under newly formed U.S. Army Research, Development and Engineering Command (Provisional) in Edgewood, Md.
October 2003	U.S. Army Integrated Materiel Management Center (IMMC) transferred to the Headquarters, U.S. Tank-Automotive and Armaments Command (TACOM) Provisional.
October 2003	Natick Garrison established under Installation Management Agency of the Northeast Region based in Virginia. All organizations are tenants of the Soldier Systems Center installation.

TENANTS OF THE U.S. ARMY SOLDIER SYSTEMS CENTER

U.S. Army Natick Soldier Center
U.S. Army Research Institute of Environmental Medicine
U.S. Navy Clothing and Textile Research Facility
U.S. Coast Guard Clothing Design and Technical Office
Program Executive Office (PEO) Soldier, PEO Combat Support–Combat Service Support, and PEO Chemical Biological Defense teams
U.S. Army Product Manager, Force Sustainment Systems
U.S. Army Installation Management Agency, Northeast Regional Office
U.S. Army Integrated Materiel Management Center
U.S. Army Robert Morris Acquisition Center, Natick
U.S. Army Soldier Systems Center, Natick

Sources: Thomas Kean, Deborah Cobban, Mike Statkus, Rose Salem, Chris Joyce, and Patty Welsh. (Reprinted from U.S. Army documents with permission.)

One

A LAB IN NATICK

Natick, now thought of primarily as a suburb of Boston, has a past that includes extensive industrialization. In particular, the town was a major site for shoe manufacturing. Some of this industry spilled over into the southern, Cochituate end of the town of Wayland. In addition to shoes, the town also hosted railroad yards, tanneries, chemical companies, a paper mill, and even an automobile factory.

The 78-acre site chosen to host the new Quartermaster Research and Development Command at Natick was on an attractive peninsula that jutted out into Lake Cochituate, a former water source for the Boston metropolis and home to a state park. The site was purchased by the U.S. Army in 1949 from the Metropolitan District Commission. The land was forested and was used primarily for recreation, but also included a gravel pit.

As the Natick Labs were being constructed and as sprawling suburban tracts were being developed within the town, this industrial mix was expanded with the addition of a Carling brewery on the opposite side of Lake Cochituate.

Since that time, the Natick Labs property has grown to include 124 buildings in Natick and surrounding communities. Included are administration, laboratory, maintenance, storage, and housing facilities, as well as stores, barbershops, a cafeteria, a credit union, and a recreation center. Special facilities include the Doriot Climatic Chambers, an altitude chamber, a textile facility, combat rations production and packaging facilities, a biomechanics lab, a three-dimensional anthropometric lab, a camouflage analysis and demo lab, a rain court, a hydroenvironmental chamber, a shade room, a fiber plant, a thermal and flame test lab, and the Military Operation in Urban Terrain (MOUT) lab.

This photograph of the main gate to the Natick Labs was taken in 1956, when a number of buildings were still incomplete.

A bulldozer and grader are shown on the construction site at Natick. Along Route 27 in the background can be seen a smokestack of a manufacturing plant, now Natick Paperboard.

In this November 1953 photograph, workers are completing a chimney for one of the lab buildings.

Another view shows workers apparently preparing the ground for building footings.

A cable-operated backhoe sits in the midst of a building foundation. In the background, a truck with a built-in derrick appears ready to hoist components into place.

With the structural steel in place, workers begin to enclose a structure with a concrete-block wall.

14

With one structure apparently complete, construction proceeds on a matching structure in the foreground. Nearly a dozen picnic tables seem ready to welcome a full staff complement.

This view looks south along Route 27 during construction of the labs. A sign on a utility pole directs drivers to the right to the U.S. Army. To the left of this intersection is the oldest house in Natick, the Bacon House, which was built in 1704.

An old Sterling chain-drive, ready-mix concrete truck from Rosenfeld Concrete, a Milford-based company, makes a delivery at the lab site.

The interior of a poured-concrete foundation or utility space is shown in this image.

A worker, identified as F. Murphy, completes installation of underground pipes to a furnace structure. A small arrow near his hand points to a water-supply pipe protruding from the ground, while the sewer pipes are at his feet.

A parked grader at the construction site overlooks a supply of angled concrete blocks, which were probably used to construct underground drains and culverts.

Tractors, a load of pipes, and a small site bulldozer are parked here behind one of the first finished lab buildings.

Here, roadwork is being completed by a crew along the shore of Lake Cochituate.

Route 27 (in the background with the railroad grade crossing) is visible in this view of the incomplete access road (Kansas Street). Note that some of the angled concrete blocks shown earlier have been used here to construct drainage revetments on each side of the road.

A utility trench is under construction in this view.

Site grading continues in this view looking southeast. The embankment of the railroad can be seen in the background.

The administration building appears to be near completion in this photograph.

A temporary shelter stands watch at one of the lab gates.

Steel reinforcing bars await forms and concrete in the foreground. In the background, various worker vehicles await the return of their owners.

The flag flies over the Natick Labs in this view. Much construction clearly remains to be done. Storage buildings are in the foreground.

The climatic building, still under construction, is seen from the roof of the administration building on December 2, 1953.

The administration building is viewed from the front of the climatic building.

In this view of the climatic building, workers install fan sections of the Doriot Climatic Chambers (a kind of wind tunnel). The building is also being painted with aluminum paint on the exterior surface to cut down on transmission of heat from sunlight.

An engineering model shows the overall plan for construction of the Natick facility.

Two

A CORNUCOPIA
OF SCIENCE

One of the many U.S. Army programs that got its start in World War II was the investigation of *trichoderma viride*, a fungus that destroyed the tents and other cotton gear during campaigns in New Guinea. The fungus had the ability to convert cellulose in cotton into glucose. The cellulose-glucose investigation was one of the first problems tackled by the new Quartermaster Laboratories. In an outgrowth of this work, Natick researchers irradiated the fungus to create a mutant strain (the first life form ever patented) that made the chemical transition even more efficiently. The technology was eventually transferred to the Department of Energy as a possible step in large-scale methanol production.

Another early initiative that involved Natick began during the Korean War. A $250,000 textile program was initiated by the Quartermaster Corps to focus on the requirements of cold climates. The effort was led by Dr. Stephen J. Kenney, who had begun his career in private industry at Pacific Mills in Lawrence. During World War II, he served in the textile section of the War Production Board. Kenney served as research director of the Clothing and Personnel Life Support Equipment Laboratory at Natick until he retired in 1973. Later, in a second career, he became a pastor of the Carter Memorial Methodist Church in Needham.

Photographs in this section include many taken at Natick, as well as some taken at affiliated and predecessor organizations during the late 1940s and early 1950s. In most cases, this work (and often, the people) ended up at Natick even if they began elsewhere.

This post–World War II display highlights the vast array of products developed under the auspices of the Quartermaster Corps.

This exhibit showcases "textile functional finishes" on uniforms and undergarments.

Frank J. Rizzo, chief of the Color Applications Branch of the Quartermaster Corps, speaks before a group that includes Colonel Dennis (sixth from right, in uniform), chief of the Research and Development Division, Office of the Quartermaster General, and Dr. A. Stuart Hunter (fifth from right), scientific director of the Research and Development Division, Office of the Quartermaster General.

Research personnel tour the Quartermaster Laboratories at Philadelphia under the guidance of Lt. Colonel Collins (second from right).

Quartermaster General Herman Feldman (left) and Command General Hugh Bryan Hester of the Philadelphia Quartermaster Depot are shown here.

A microscopy preparation laboratory at the Natick Labs is shown here. The facility acquired an RCA electron microscope capable of magnifying objects 100,000 times in size.

General Hester gets a closeup view of lab work in Philadelphia.

A Natick researcher inserts a specimen for analysis in the RCA electron microscope.

A more traditional microscopy technique is shown here: a camera focused through an optical microscope.

Another of the lab's new tools was this Bard Associates infrared recording spectrophotometer, manufactured in Cambridge, Massachusetts. The lab also boasted a Beckman spectrophotometer and a Hunter multipurpose reflectometer. All were useful for a variety of applications in materials science.

The lab had yet another spectrophotometer, this one made by General Electric. Here a researcher studies the output chart from the instrument.

Reviewing output charts in the days before computerization required hands-on analysis and the hand-recording of data.

This more traditional scene not only shows researchers with their sleeves rolled up in a figurative sense but also showcases the refined dress code of the 1950s.

A vacuum distillation process is harnessed by lab researchers for a study of enzymes.

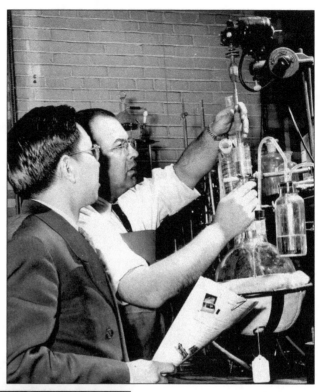

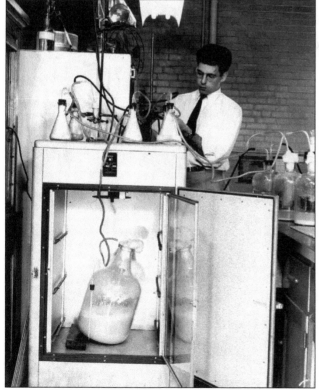

While resembling an experiment gone awry—according to a scrapbook caption—this view actually shows a "method of preparation for a substrate material prior to isolating active enzymes derived from degrading fungi."

33

Enzymes could also be derived from this "alternative" setup. Note the man with the rubberized or leather apron, apparently prepared for the worst.

The lab maintained scores of mosquito colonies that were used in research efforts to reduce the hazards to U.S. personnel from this ubiquitous source of misery.

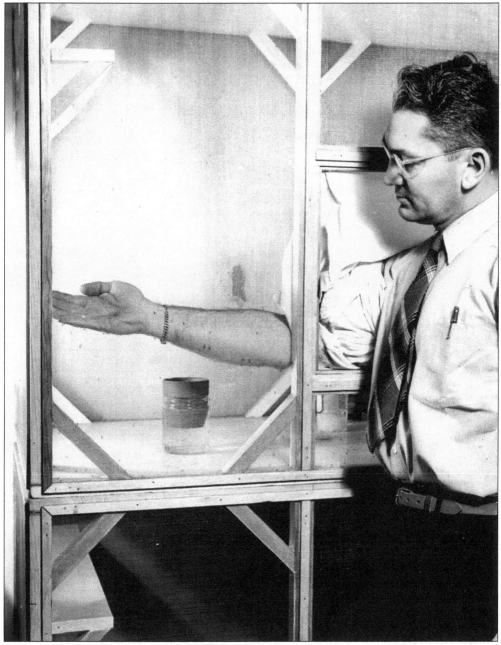

Epitomizing the notion of suffering for a good cause, a researcher assures the survival of a brood of mosquitoes by offering up his arm as a feeding station.

Army records describe this view as "color comparison for biological studies on fungi."

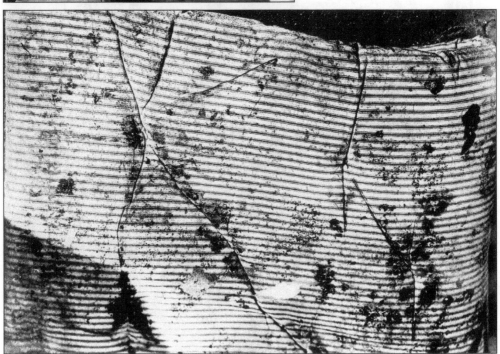

Army life is no bed of roses for the average soldier. However, this experiment studying the impact of mold in deteriorating standard bedding was designed to ensure improved comfort and longer service life for equipment.

A researcher examines the content of a petri dish.

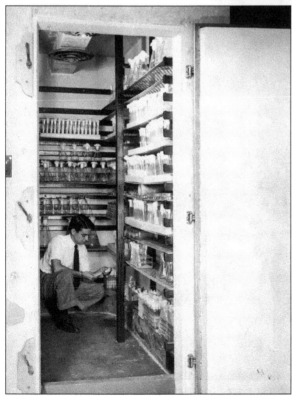

To ensure the success of its experiments, Natick set up this walk-in incubation chamber for fungi studies.

Understanding fungi demanded more than just looking at the slime in petri dishes. Here, a researcher uses a Warburg manometer while conducting respiratory studies on fungi.

This photograph shows the inoculation of agar plates for isolating and identifying fungi.

This photograph shows the feed end of a plastic coating machine, probably in Philadelphia. Natick researchers were pioneers in applying new polymers to a variety of equipment needs.

The photographer caught the middle of a run for a pre-pilot plant to manufacture fine filaments of glass and plastic. Dr. Ralph G. H. Siu, director of the General Laboratories, is on the ground level, speaking with Dr. Rolf K. Ladisch, on the platform.

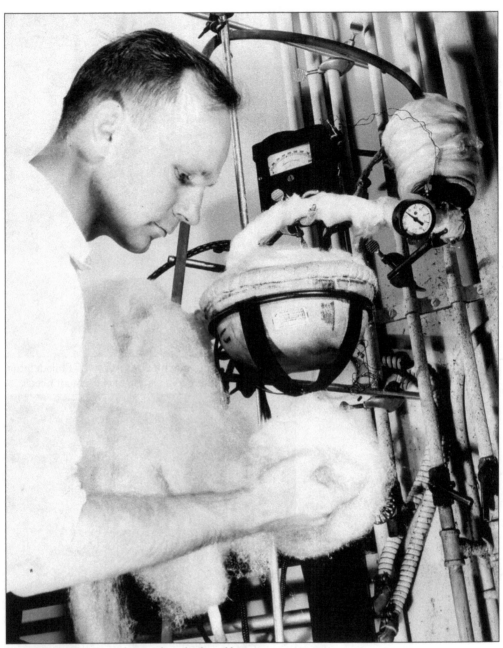

Dr. Ladisch examines the results of a fine-filament experiment.

These test strips of soil-burial samples show the efficiency of various fungicidal treatments.

Songwriter George M. Cohan made famous the lament of soldiers who hate to get up in the morning. This test setup ensured that soldiers' cots would be able to support them all night long—no matter what. Here, the impact of a tired soldier "hitting the sack" at full speed is simulated with an appropriately weighted device. Obviously, this cot did not measure up.

The Men Working sign at the left seems to mock the strange but necessary task performed by these laboratory personnel—in this case, walking for hours in rain gear in a simulated storm.

Sharing knowledge was a key component of the lab's mission. Here, a lecturer discusses the frustrating phenomenon of fabric shrinkage. The display shows an untreated wool sweater (badly shrunken after 10 launderings) and a special "resin-treated" sweater that has resisted shrinking.

This facility tested textiles for shrinkage and other wear issues.

Out-of-doors testing was also a crucial element in ensuring high-quality equipment. Here, a field test exposes different fabrics to simulated rainfall.

Another of the detailed tests conducted by lab personnel was the drop-penetration test for treated cloth. The test was designed to determine the efficiency of waterproofing treatments.

Long-range storage test chambers were used to ensure the stability and durability of a variety of materials. In this case, leather is being tested in three different chambers: a hot and dry "desert" storage facility, a hot and wet "tropical" storage facility, and a "moderate summer" storage facility.

Color was also an important characteristic of army equipment. Here, in experimental dye baths, small samples of yarn are tested in individual dye pots.

Two pilot plant "padders" are used to apply dyestuff to cloth by mechanical means.

Believe it or not, this machine really was called a fade-o-meter. It contained a carbon arc lamp of fixed intensity around which small samples revolved for a specific exposure time. The device, in which 50 hours of exposure equaled three months' exposure to sunlight, allowed for rapid acceleration in testing fabrics and other material.

This tensile tester, built by Route 128–based Instron, provided a constant rate of load and was used to measure the breaking strength of fabric. The apparatus was so sensitive that it could be used to record the breaking strength of individual fibers.

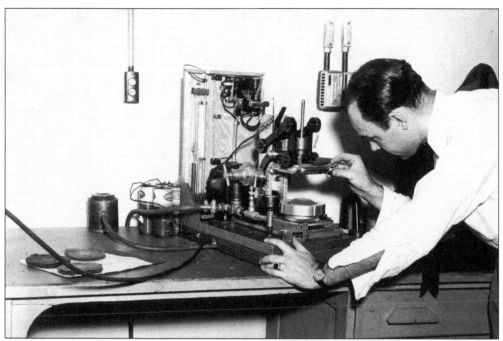

As if fading and weather were not enough of a test for textiles, the lab also employed this Stoll abrader (developed by Dr. R. G. Stoll, a lab employee) to test the abrasion resistance of materials.

Seen here is another Stoll abrader, as produced commercially for use in other laboratories around the country.

This modified plunger-type burst tester was used to measure the strength of leather.

Technicians enter a subzero test chamber maintained at negative 60 degrees Fahrenheit.

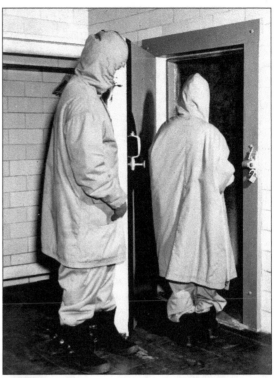

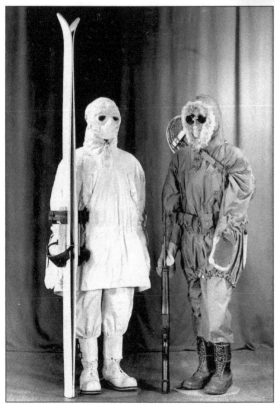

These are examples of early arctic clothing developed by the Quartermaster Laboratories.

49

Plastic- and rubber-coated fabrics were used to develop air mattresses.

This taupe hat was the height of fashion for army nurses and served as part of the 1951–1953 service uniform. The design of uniforms remains part of the work at the Natick Labs to this day.

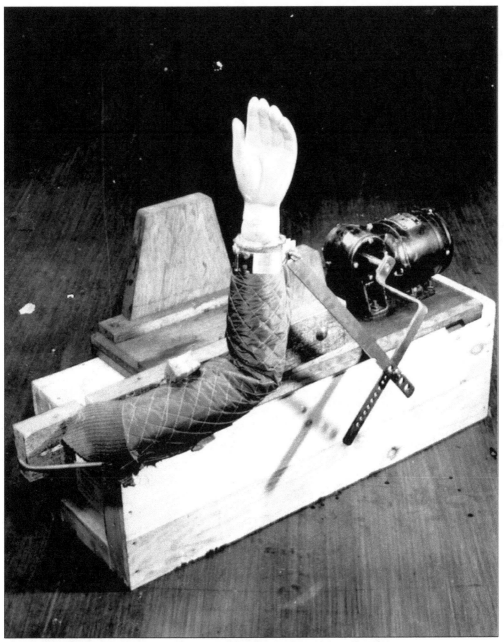

This apparatus was developed to determine flexing qualities of insulated garments.

The Maeser Walking Water Penetration Machine was used to determine the effectiveness of waterproofing applications on leather shoes.

A lab technician performs preventive maintenance and modifications on electronic instruments.

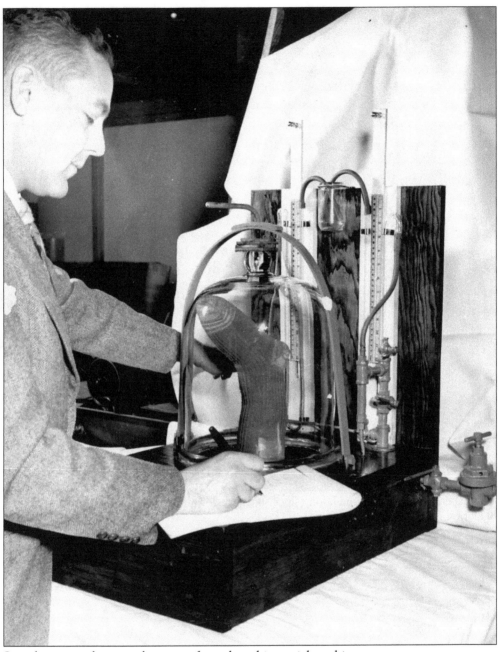

Stretch testing of army socks was performed on this special machine.

This experimental wind tunnel, long since superseded, was used to test the wind-permeability of fabrics.

Three

LAUNCHING A LAB

In 1947, two bills were introduced in Congress to authorize a move of the Quartermaster Corps research facilities to the New England region. Although objections from other regions helped to slow the measure (some 278 alternate proposals from 40 states were eventually considered), the combination of the region's attractions and its effective political leadership finally led to approval of a facility in Natick on March 8, 1951. The ceremonial laying of a cornerstone took place on May 30, 1953, with Speaker Joseph W. Martin Jr., Sen. Leverett Saltonstall, Sen. John F. Kennedy, and others in attendance. Finally, the dedication of the facility, pictured in this section, occurred on October 14, 1954.

In an article entitled "The New Quartermaster Research & Development Command," which appeared in the July–August 1954 edition of the *Quartermaster Review*, Brig. Gen. J. C. Odell wrote:

> At the present time the Command has somewhat over 100 active research and development projects aimed at the improvement of items for soldier use. Most of these projects are conducted with the participation and/or coordination of 22 other government agencies, principally the Army Field Forces, the Air Force, all the Technical Services, the Office of the Surgeon General, the Navy; the Ordnance, Signal and Chemical Corps; and the Atomic Energy Commission.
>
> Under the supervision of the Command's scientific and technological staff, many of the projects are farmed out under contracts to leading industrial and university laboratories where special kinds of technical information are known to be located. These contracts number 250, and range in size from $3,000 to upwards of $100,000. One project may have a number of contracts outlying. For example, there are eleven universities at work on a single project.
>
> The new Center has made a good start. A strong nucleus of Quartermaster scientific and technological personnel has made the move to Natick, and a serious lag in the work has been avoided.
>
> It is evident that the choice of Natick, in the metropolitan Boston area, as the site for this research-and-development activity was guided by long-range foresight. In this community, many of the country's greatest universities, with unlimited reservoirs of scientific information, are located. On these we may freely draw, at the same time renewing cooperative contacts already made and establishing additional fact-finding bases, both in the research stockpiles of educational institutions and in those of nearby industrial concerns.

Members of the 18th U.S. Army Band and the color guard from Fort Devens enter the site for the dedication of the Quartermaster Research and Development Command at Natick. The Quartermaster facility was dedicated on October 14, 1954. Robert T. Stevens, secretary of the army, made the principal address.

A substantial crowd gathered to witness the dedication and to hear the dignitaries.

On his arrival at the dedication ceremony, Maj. Gen. E. C. Plow (commanding general, Eastern Command, Canadian Army) is greeted by Eleanor Hall, a hostess for the event.

In this view, Maj. Gen. E. C. Plow (second from left) is greeted by Maj. William T. Molloy (far left) of the U.S. Army.

Robert T. Stevens, secretary of the army, addresses the crowd. Seated are, from left to right, Rev. Richard A. Strong of St. Paul's Episcopal Church, Natick; Joseph W. Martin, Speaker of the House of Representatives; Sen. Leverett Saltonstall, chairman of the House Armed Services Committee; Brig. Gen. Charles G. Calloway, commanding general of the Quartermaster Research and Development Command; Maj. Gen. Kester L. Hastings, the quartermaster general; and Rep. John W. McCormack.

Rev. Joseph M. Holland of St. Patrick's Roman Catholic Church, Natick, delivered the benediction at the dedication ceremony.

This photograph captures the salute to the colors during the dedication ceremony.

Shown here is the presentation of the colors during the ceremony.

Col. Russell K. Kuhns (left), deputy for administration at the Quartermaster Research and Development Command, and Donald J. Hurley, president of the Boston Chamber of Commerce, chat during the festivities.

Maj. Gen. L. E. Simon (chief of the Research and Development Division, Ordnance Corps) is seen entering the administration building. Maj. A. E. Edmonston is to the left.

Guests arrive at the administration building.

Brig. Gen. H. R. McKenzie, comptroller of the Office of the Quartermaster General, and his wife arrive at the administration building. Maj. H. D. Shewmaker is to the right.

Shown from left to right are Dr. A. Stuart Hunter, scientific director at the Quartermaster center; Robert T. Stevens, secretary of the army; Maj. Gen. Kester L. Hastings; and Maj. Gen. Charles G. Calloway. Hunter, the facility's first scientific director, supervised a wide range of activities at Natick as well as at the Field Evaluation Agency (in Fort Lee) and the Food and Container Institute (in Chicago). He died while at work in October 1958.

From left to right are Joseph W. Martin Jr., Speaker of the House of Representatives; Donald A. Quarles, assistant secretary of defense for research and development; Maj. Gen. E. C. Plow; Sen. Leverett Saltonstall; Robert T. Stevens, secretary of the army; Maj. Gen. Kester L. Hastings; and Maj. Gen. Charles G. Calloway, commander of the new $11 million facility.

U.S. Rep. Joseph W. Martin Jr., Speaker of the House, addresses the crowd of approximately 2,000 people.

Frank H. Higgins, assistant secretary of defense, and his wife enter the administration building, accompanied by Brig. Gen. A. B. Denniston (immediately behind Mr. Higgins).

Massachusetts congressman John W. McCormack, who later became Speaker of the House of Representatives, eyes the crowd.

Maj. Gen. A. L. Marshall (left), commanding general of the Quartermaster Market Center System (the purchasing organization for the army's fresh and preserved foods), talks with Col. Russell K. Kuhns, deputy for administration at the Quartermaster Research and Development Command.

Frank H. Higgins (center), assistant secretary of the army, and his wife are greeted by Maj. Gen. Kester L. Hastings (right).

In this view, dignitaries applaud the secretary of the army, Robert T. Stevens.

Maj. Gen. (Retired) Sanford Jarman, at center, is seen entering the administration building.

The color guard marches into position for ceremonies.

Some of the 2,000 attendees at the dedication ceremony are shown in this view.

Maj. C. G. Adams (second from left) and Maj. H. D. Shewmaker (far right) greet Rear Adm. John A. Snackenberg (center), commandant of the 1st Naval District, upon his arrival.

Robert T. Stevens, secretary of the army, addresses the radio audience of WKOX, a Framingham-based station.

Brigadier J. W. Bishop (commander, Canadian Army Staff), on right, is seen as he enters the administration building with Brigadier R. W. Ewbanks (British Joint Service Mission) and Ewbanks's wife.

Below the flag, one can glimpse Frank H. Higgins (assistant secretary of the army), at far left, and Brig. Gen. A. B. Denniston. The group on the right includes Robert T. Stephens, secretary of the army; Brig. Gen. Charles G. Calloway; Rep. John W. McCormack; and Richard Preston, commissioner of welfare for Massachusetts.

On October 23, 1954, a few days after the dedication ceremony, special ceremonies were held at the office of the acting quartermaster general, Maj. Gen. Kester L. Hastings (front row, second from left). Awards of merit and certificates of honorable mention were presented to six scientists and technologists. From left to right are the following: (first row) Dr. A. Stuart Hunter, technical director at Natick; Maj. Gen. Kester L. Hastings; Col. W. D. Jackson, chief, Research and Development Division; Albert W. Drobile, chief, Industrial Fabrics Engineering Unit, Textile Materials Engineering Laboratory, Philadelphia; (second row) Dr. Thaddeus C. Kmiecjak, technologist, Production Branch, Quartermaster Food and Container Institute for the Armed Forces, Chicago Quartermaster Depot; Dr. George Susich, fiber technologist, Research and Development Textile Laboratory, Philadelphia Quartermaster Depot; Dr. David F. Bass, director, Biochemistry Section, Quartermaster Climatic Research Laboratory, Lawrence; James R. Aldridge, designer, Textile Equipage Products Division, Jeffersonville Quartermaster Depot (Indiana); and Alexander C. Weiss, plastics technologist, Chemicals and Plastics Branch, Research and Development Division, Office of the Quartermaster General, Washington, D.C.

Four

DECADES OF

INNOVATION

Over the years, Natick researchers have played a leading role in the development of many new technologies. Starting in the mid-1950s, with the Atoms for Peace program, Natick investigated food irradiation for both military and civilian purposes. Natick led in the development of freeze-dried foods, as well as the many "space foods" used by NASA (the National Aeronautics and Space Administration).

One of the most famous of Natick innovators was Australian Sir Hubert Wilkins, a renowned arctic explorer and authority on polar and desert regions. He worked as a geographer and climatologist for the Quartermaster Corps starting in World War II, and subsequently was employed as a geographer by the Environmental Protection Research Division, at Quartermaster Research and Engineering Command, Natick. Wilkins died in his room at the Park Central Hotel in Framingham on November 30, 1958.

One of the most visible facilities at Natick for many years was the giant heliostat (solar furnace) located close to the shore of Lake Cochituate. Its reflective surfaces were capable of producing intense concentrations of solar energy that could simulate the thermal effects of nuclear explosions. For instance, the mirrors could generate temperatures of up to 7,000 degrees Fahrenheit—easily sufficient to burn holes through large pieces of steel. At lower temperatures, according to some sources, the facility was used to test sunscreen-like lotions on animals in a quest to produce substances that could better protect American soldiers and civilians from the effect of nuclear blasts. The equipment was later transferred to White Sands, New Mexico, in the early 1970s to take advantage of more reliable sunlight.

By 1965, the labs employed some 1,600 civilians, a third of whom were scientists or engineers.

This aerial view, taken not long after the opening of the Natick Labs, clearly shows the spectacular location along the shores of Lake Cochituate. In the middle ground and to the left

can be seen buildings projects still under way.

This photograph, taken on the morning of October 5, 1954, shows a large Class A fire being extinguished by booster lines from town of Natick fire equipment.

A large oil fire in a 15-foot-wide pit is put out using two Ansul dry-chemical extinguishers in this demonstration event. In the era before environmental regulations, such cavalier handling of petroleum and chemicals was nearly universal. In the case of the Natick Labs, it has led to serious long-term environmental problems on and near the site.

After the demonstration put on by the General Equipment Company, personnel pose for the camera. From left to right are Maj. H. A. Fillmer, fire marshal; J. E. Ferrick, fire inspector; Deputy Chief B. W. Glebus, Natick Fire Department; and Daniel McKay and a colleague, identified as Mr. Marvel, both of General Equipment.

This mid-1950s view shows the lab-affiliated Quartermaster Research and Development Command, Mount Washington Test Detachment. The extremes of climate around New England's highest peak provided an ideal test environment.

Observers at a Mount Washington winter test in 1949 already give example of the interservice cooperation often to be demonstrated at the Natick Labs. From left to right are the following: (first row) Maxine Spengler, Office of the Quartermaster General; Lt. Col. Katherine Baltz, Army Nurse Corps; Capt. M. Moran, Women in the Air Force; and Lieutenant Burt, Signal Corps; (second row) Maj. J. E. Barnhill, Office of the Quartermaster General; Col. Emma Vogel, Women's Medical Specialist Corps; Lt. Frances E. Quebbeman, Navy Nurse Corps; Capt. Gioia Toy, Office of the Quartermaster General; and Lt. Carl Ashline, Quartermaster Corps.

Test subjects are shown here clad in men's experimental arctic clothing. The two on the left are wearing parkas and trousers as outer garments. The two on the right are wearing jackets and trousers. All are wearing arctic felt boots.

Test subjects are outfitted with women's standard cold-climate clothing. The two on the left are wearing a parka-type overcoat and trousers. The two on the right are wearing field jackets with hoods. All are wearing women's arctic overshoes.

The star of Natick's efforts to develop improved cold-weather gear was Sir Hubert Wilkins, seen at the microphone in this undated image. Wilkins, who consulted in various capacities to the U.S. government starting early in World War II, had been involved in a number of arctic expeditions, and once even commanded the first submarine to travel under the icecap—a privately funded craft called the *Nautilus* (which predated its famous nuclear successor by a generation). In one incident, a local policeman found Wilkins sleeping by the railroad tracks one winter evening. Why was Wilkins there? He was personally testing a new chicken feather–filled sleeping bag under development at Natick. Wilkins resided in Framingham until his death in 1958.

This image from the 1980s shows the variety of snowshoes that were evaluated by Natick.

Field tests still play a part in qualifying clothing and equipment. This undated photograph shows the outside temperature (57 degrees below zero) on a lab venture to Alaska.

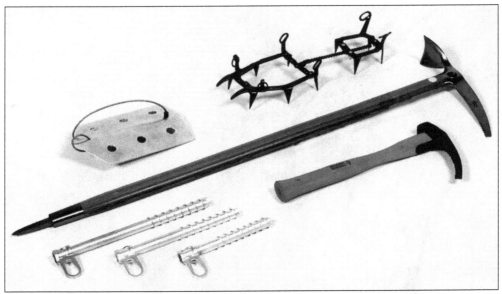

Crampons, ice axes, and other paraphernalia of winter survival also came in for scrutiny at the Natick Labs.

Perhaps not fashionable but certainly effective, this equipment was developed or tested at Natick. Note the white camouflage applied over the clothing.

And after a tough day of skiing with a full pack and an M-16, a hot meal (in this case, rice and chicken) is bound to be a morale booster.

82

Afternoon traffic exits the Natick Labs property not long after the facility opened. Note the dirt road surface and an early Volkswagen in the parking lot at the right.

In this 1950s photograph, John Slauta (left), Bob Woodbury (center), and George Schneider prepare to test survival suits in the Pentagon Lagoon. The Washington Monument can be glimpsed in the distance.

For a good cause, the three men seen in the previous view (apparently joined by a fourth) make the most of the flotation and warmth provided by their suits.

Back on dry land after the test, the same three men showcase the workings of their equipment.

One result of the research exemplified in the previous views was the U.S. Navy–Marine Corps immersion suit, designed to provide a disposable form of water protection for soldiers, particularly for use during amphibious assaults.

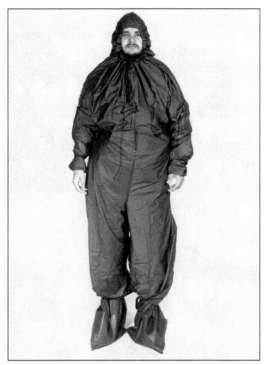

This illustration, used by the Natick Labs, highlights the challenges facing military food suppliers—the need to produce high-quality food that can be delivered and served under the most challenging circumstances.

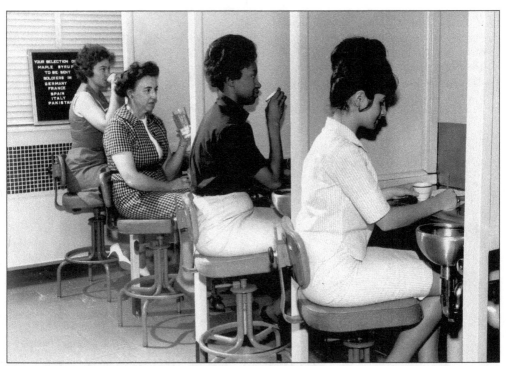

These women have the sweetest job at the Natick Labs. They are taste-testing maple-syrup samples for use by the armed forces. Note the sinks beside each booth for disposing of samples.

Researcher Pat Prell examines a food sample in this 1969 photograph.

Gen. William Westmoreland (second from left) visits the Natick Labs in this 1969 photograph. (The man on the left and two generals on the right are not identified.)

During his visit General Westmoreland (center) samples some rations developed at the Natick Labs. (The other men in the photograph are not identified.)

With Lake Cochituate in the background, this soldier demonstrates food rehydration.

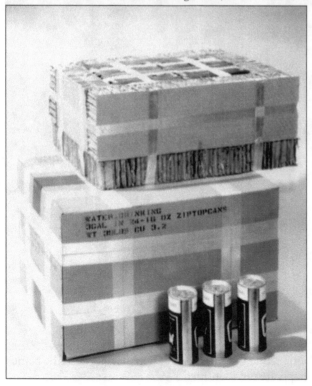
This 1967 photograph shows the packaging used to protect canned water rations.

Freeze-drying, a pioneering development by the Natick Labs, was quickly implemented in civilian products such as Tang and Maxim.

This *c.* 1980 photograph shows a sample of freeze-dried vegetables. The freeze-drying process, pioneered by Natick, allowed 34 servings to be packed into a single can.

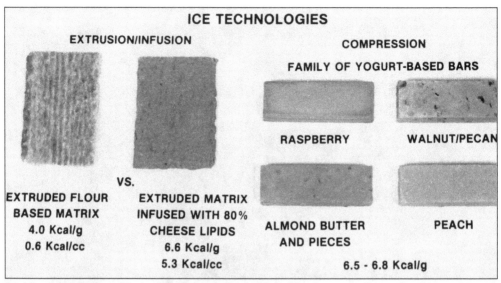

ICE TECHNOLOGIES

EXTRUSION/INFUSION

COMPRESSION

FAMILY OF YOGURT-BASED BARS

VS.

EXTRUDED FLOUR BASED MATRIX
4.0 Kcal/g
0.6 Kcal/cc

EXTRUDED MATRIX INFUSED WITH 80% CHEESE LIPIDS
6.6 Kcal/g
5.3 Kcal/cc

RASPBERRY

WALNUT/PECAN

ALMOND BUTTER AND PIECES

PEACH

6.5 - 6.8 Kcal/g

Packing lots of nutrition (preferably in a flavorful form) into a small area has been a Natick obsession. This illustration identifies a variety of formulations and production methods.

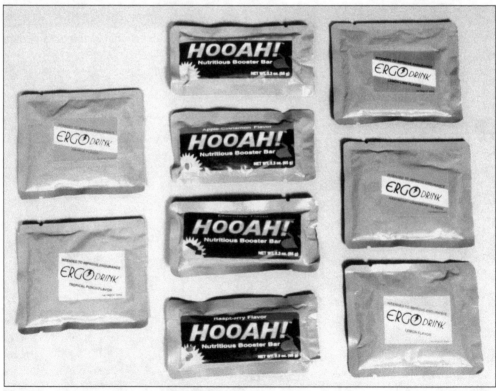

The Hooah bar, a nutritious snack food, and Ergo Drink are two results of Natick's long devotion to food development. Both were developed to enhance the cognitive and physical endurance of the individual soldier. According to the U.S. Army, these products contain the right proportions of complex carbohydrates that convert to energy-rich glucose and specific amino acids to help minimize stress-induced impairment of performance.

An unidentified soldier samples Natick food c. 1973.

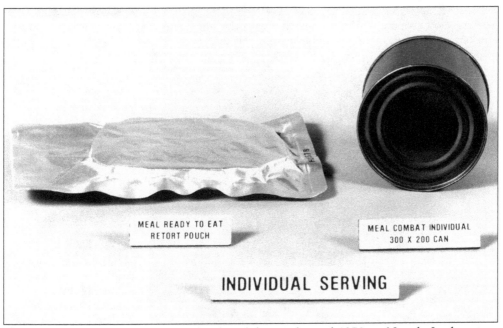

MEAL READY TO EAT
RETORT POUCH

MEAL COMBAT INDIVIDUAL
300 X 200 CAN

INDIVIDUAL SERVING

The MRE (meal ready to eat) was developed during the mid-1970s at Natick. In this view, an MRE is contrasted with a typical canned product. The pouch allowed a greater variety of food products to be made available. The meals were introduced to military personnel in the early 1980s.

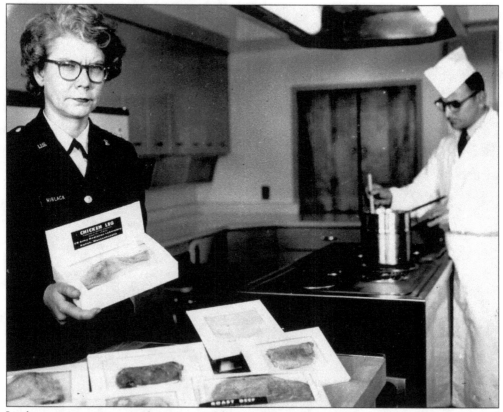

Looking most serious, a military researcher with the surname Niblack shows off an irradiated chicken leg. Irradiation was researched extensively by Natick.

Shown here is a pepper treated by irradiation—another of the lab's explorations that had civilian repercussions. Irradiation of fresh produce such as strawberries is now widely practiced in the food industry.

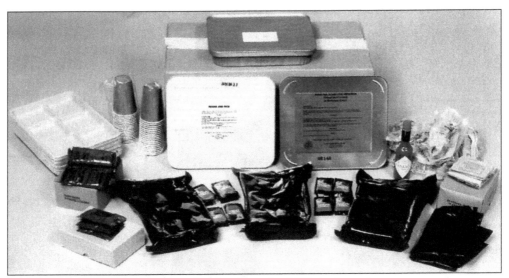

A CFD (combat feeding directorate) ration from the 1980s is shown here.

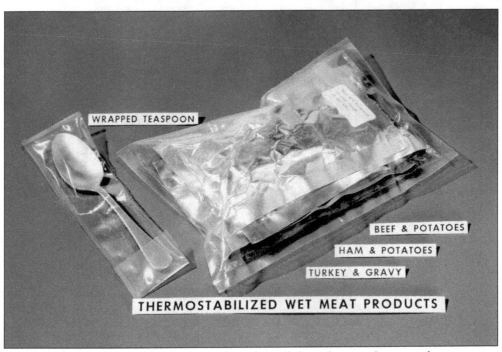

Thermostabilized wet meat products were Natick breakthroughs in packaging and processing.

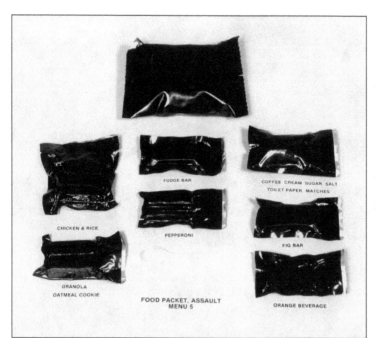

Foods for use under assault conditions were developed for this army-issue food packet.

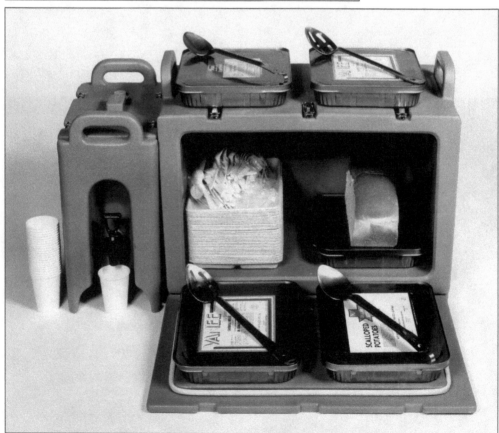

Insulated food containers allowed first-class food to be served on the front lines.

Carol Tucker Foreman (left), assistant secretary of agriculture during the Carter administration, and Massachusetts congresswoman Margaret M. Heckler (center), of Wellesley, concentrate while tasting samples of irradiated bacon during their visit to Natick's Food Engineering Laboratory in February 1979. Dr. Dale H. Sieling (center background), technical director of the lab, observes the test while Dr. Hamed M. El-Bisi, deputy technical director, offers samples.

Looking over rations in this photograph are individuals affiliated with the Natick Labs. From left to right are Maj. Joe Demby, Abner Salant, Justin Toomey, Nick Montanerelli, and Rauno Lampey.

Natick's influence also extended to development of field cooking equipment. Here, forward-area troops are being served garrison-type food with the help of an MFS (mobile food service) unit, in the background.

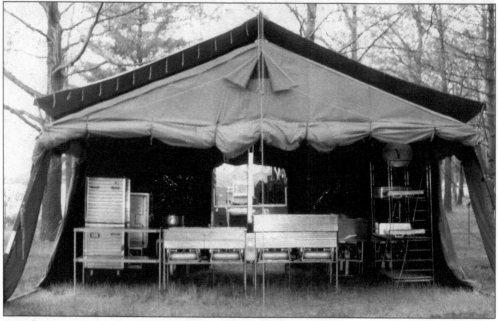

Seen here is a mobile field kitchen set up at Natick.

The interior of a mobile lavatory is shown in this view.

This mobile laundry on a trailer was developed with the help of the Natick Labs.

Several styles of pup tents are being tested outside a Natick building.

Large tents undergo tests on a strip of lawn at Natick.

A soldier uses a mobile laundry station.

A mobile facility is deployed beside Lake Cochituate.

This photograph, probably taken in Bosnia in 1996, shows a number of mobile systems developed by Natick being used in the field.

An army Jeep, probably from the 1970s, is being readied to "disappear" with the application of a polymer foam.

The expanding polymer foam has turned the Jeep into an irregularly shaped object that is hard to recognize even at close range.

Another disappearing act comes courtesy of a reflective sheet (in the foreground) that is stretched in front of an already camouflaged object.

This shot could be called "stress for success." In a number of labs similar to this, personnel could be tested under a variety of temperature conditions. Here, in a recent image, several men are monitored while wearing varying levels of clothing and equipment.

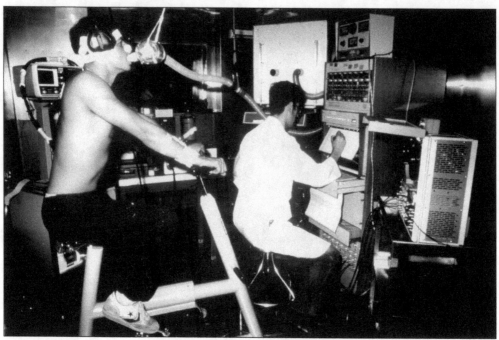

This test looks at a variety of physiological responses. Not only is respiration monitored, but the subject also has a syringe hanging from his arm for taking blood samples.

Here, personnel at the Army Research Institute of Environmental Medicine (ARIEM) monitor a subject in a test tank.

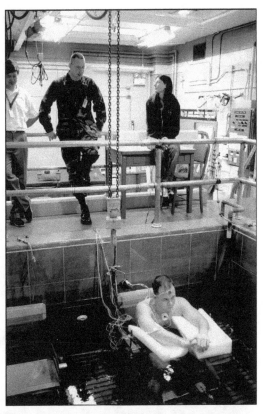

Another test subject, this one in uniform, is put through similar tests in this view.

Using technology similar to that used in an astronaut's spacesuit, Natick developed this head-cooling unit and portable refrigeration device as part of a modular cooling system. The system was designed to protect crewmen from severe thermal stresses while in combat vehicles, such as tanks.

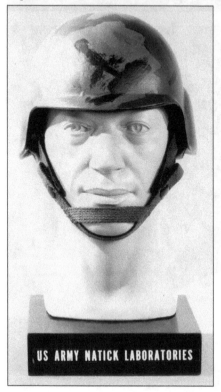

US ARMY NATICK LABORATORIES

This 1974 photograph shows a prototype of the new infantry helmet that succeeded the style used from the early 1950s on.

The new helmet was designed to be comfortable and provide good ballistics protection, as this survivor from the 1989–1990 Panama incursion demonstrates. In a few documented cases, the new helmet protected the wearer from an AK-47 round fired at close range—a greater degree of protection than it was designed to provide.

A prototype desert uniform is shown in this 1980 view.

A garment designed to provide nighttime camouflage and extra warmth covers a prototype desert uniform.

In this 1960s image, the figure in the painting seems to stare down approvingly on the woman wearing a warp-knit summer dress "with princess lines and rolled collar." The outfit was developed at Natick for optional purchase by army personnel.

Two female personnel display
Natick-crafted uniform designs,
probably in the 1950s or 1960s.

An undated raincoat design is shown here.

Three U.S. Navy personnel model Natick gear aboard CVN 74, the aircraft carrier *John C. Stennis.*

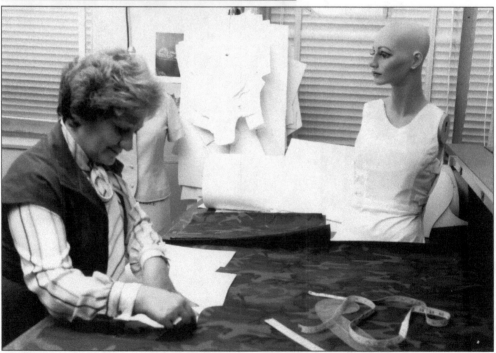

Shown on the mannequin is a designer's model of Natick-developed ballistic vest with bulletproof seam construction. The photograph is probably from the late 1970s.

This is a 1978 microscope photograph of experimental fabric for use in protective clothing. The weft-insertion, warp-knit fabric was photographed under tension to show its construction. The darker yarn is Nomex aramid yarn, which is warp knitted around weft yarn made from activated carbon yarn covered with cotton yarn.

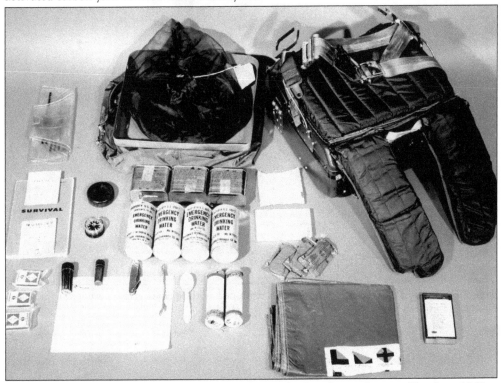

Displayed here are a Natick-developed warm-climate food packet and survival kit from 1967.

This 1978 image seems to show a uniform equipped with special grips, perhaps to facilitate removal of injured personnel.

Shown in a 1967 photograph, this harness was probably intended for aerial extraction of downed air personnel.

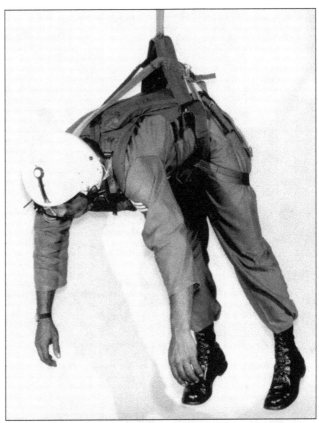

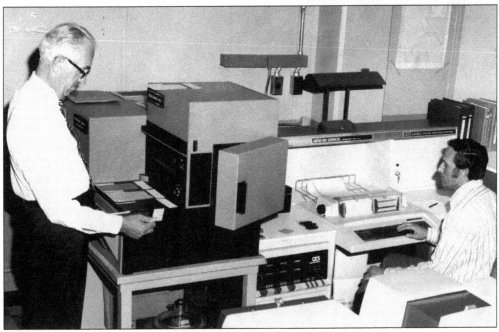

Natick technicians operate a computer-interfaced spectrophotometer to predict pigment formulations needed to match camouflage colors.

This photograph shows the U.S. Army Research Institute of Environmental Medicine (ARIEM) at Natick.

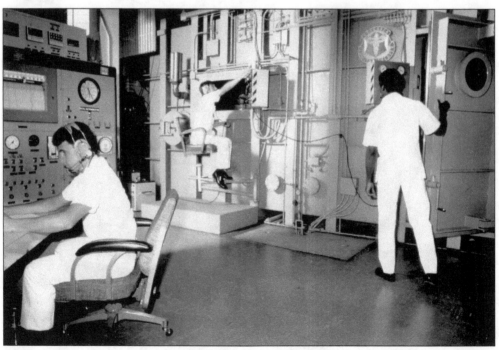

ARIEM personnel operate test chambers into which subjects are placed to test their physiological response to various environments and conditions.

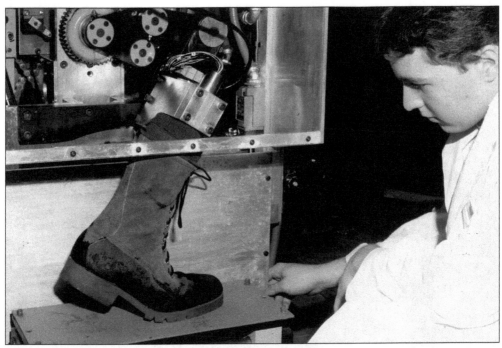

Shown is another Natick machine for testing boots.

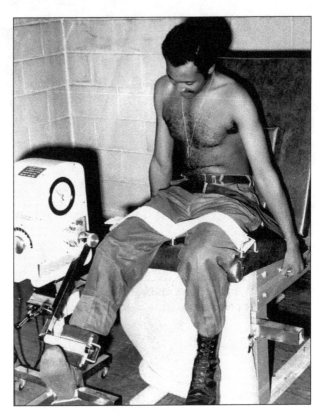

This machine appears to be measuring the human end of the boot equation.

Airdrop technologies have also been a major product of Natick. Here, a transport jettisons what appears to be prefabricated trusses or a bridge structure.

A load similar to that in the previous photograph is shown descending under several parachutes.

Here, a soldier is attired in Natick body armor developed during the Vietnam War period.

New jungle boots, designed to be resistant to the deadly punji stakes employed by the Viet Cong, were developed by the Natick Labs during the Vietnam War.

This Vietnam-era image illustrates the number and type of items carried by typical U.S. soldiers. Natick performed many studies to assess ways to streamline and systematize equipment in order to reduce stress on soldiers.

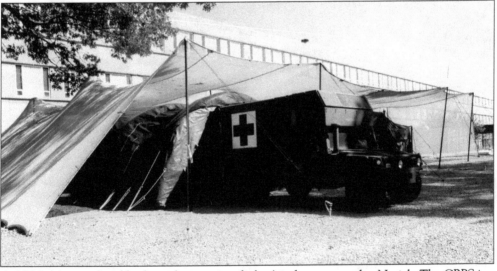

A CBPS (chemical and biological protective shelter) is demonstrated at Natick. The CBPS is a highly mobile, vehicle-mounted, rigid-wall shelter with attached chem-bio-protected, airbeam-supported tent. The unit provides an environmentally controlled work area that filters out nuclear, biological, and chemical agents. The self-deploying shelter is used as a battalion-aid station for forward medical treatment in a contaminated environment, and several CBPSs can be complexed to form a forward surgical team.

A CBPS is carried into a forward area by a Chinook helicopter.

A CBPS is shown set up in the field.

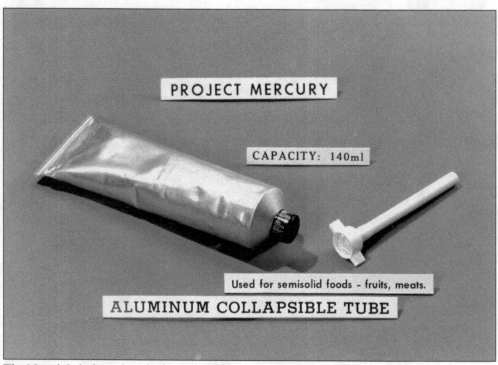

The Natick Labs have long had an intimate involvement with the space program. Here are the famous tubes of food used in weightless environments by the astronauts of the Mercury program in the early 1960s.

More recently, the Hooah bar—a tasty and nutritious snack creation from Natick—also made its way into the space program. An unidentified member of the space shuttle crew is shown here.

Pallets inside a transport aircraft are being readied for aerial offloading using a Natick-designed system.

A C-130 offloads a bulldozer (with parachutes) just above the ground.

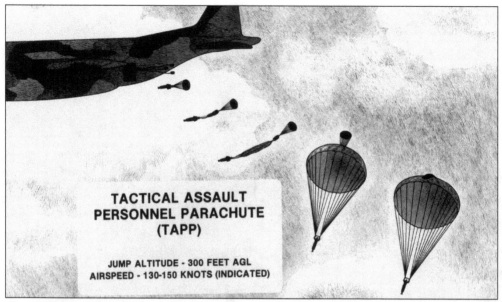

The TAPP (tactical assault personnel parachute system) is explained in this diagram. In the testing of another early parachute innovation (the high-altitude, low-opening chute system), Col. Donald L. Gellnicht, director of the Airborne Engineering Laboratory from 1971 to 1972, was killed at the Fort Devens drop zone when his own chute malfunctioned. The conference room in the headquarters building at Natick honors his memory.

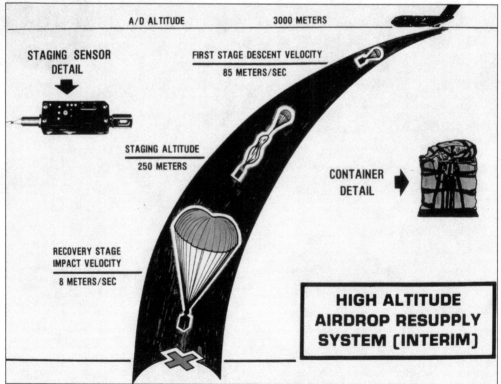

This diagram illustrates the high-altitude airdrop resupply system.

This image seems to show a TAPP recovery drop zone.

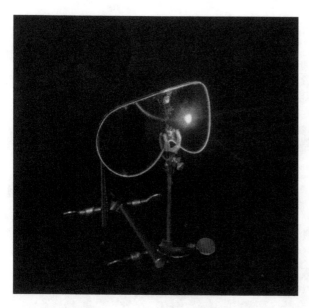

Laser protective glasses are shown here. Natick has studied the dangers of laser light since the early 1960s. In 1990, Natick helped field the first glasses designed to protect the eyes from powerful flashes of laser light. Engineers also successfully completed development of two-wavelength protective capability of the BLPS (ballistic laser protective spectacles) added to the goggles and flier's helmet visor. A three-wavelength protective capability developed for the goggles and the visor can be used for protection from sunlight and glare during daytime operations. All three laser protective devices were fielded during Operation Desert Storm.

In the 1990s, Natick was closely involved with the beginnings of the SIPE (soldier integrated protective ensemble) initiative, which was intended to improve the capabilities of dismounted soldiers to shoot, move, communicate, and survive.

From head to toe, this soldier of the 82nd Airborne Division, on deployment in Afghanistan as part of Operation Enduring Freedom, is equipped with numerous items developed by Natick over the years since its establishment.

This Coast Guardsman watching over New York's post-9/11 harbor wears a uniform developed by the Coast Guard Clothing Design and Technical Office, which is yet another element in the remarkable interservice concentration of talent at today's Soldier Systems Center at Natick.

Printed in the USA
CPSIA information can be obtained
at www.ICGtesting.com
LVHW081428251023
761775LV00009B/586